Dekeleba – the Lake Bird

The Story of Pastor Kitapateke

by

Sarah Kende

NENGE BOOKS

Dekeleba - the Lake Bird
The Story of Pastor Kitapateke

by Sarah Kende

Copyright © Sarah Kende 2020
All rights reserved.

Published by Nenge Books, Australia, March 2020
ABN 26809396184
nengebooks1@gmail.com
nengebooks.com

This book or parts thereof may not be reproduced in any form, stored in a retrieval system, or transmited in any form by any means - electronic, mechanical, photocopy, recording or otherwise - without the prior written permission of the publisher.

Photographs © Ken Macnaughtan, used by permission.

Layout, editing and cover design by Nenge Books.

This book can be purchased directly from the publisher or ordered through bookshops.

Nenge Books publishes quality books using cost effective print-on-demand technology suitable for both small and large print runs, including biographies, general interest stories, training and text books.
Enquiries to publish should be emailed to nengebooks1@gmail.com

ISBN 978-0-6484284-8-0

Contents

Dokei to Yanguli	5
The Dobu Trade	11
Arranged Marriage	15
The Lord's Calling	18
Samberigi Bible School	23
Life at the Bible School	28
First Posting	30
Retired	33

Dekeleba

*This book is dedicated to Pastor Kitapateke,
every word was his own.*

Dokei to Yanguli

It was in the 1930's when outside explorers first began penetrating the highlands of Papua New Guinea. The southern part of the country was mandated as a British colony. In the remote Southern Highlands region Kitapateke's forefathers were just embracing this enlightenment to a world outside their own and seeking to differentiate between man and the unseen world - and discover if the newcomers were real human beings! To them this was the dawning of a new era in which the stone-age was coming to an end.

Tribal wars were still inevitable as it became somewhat of a game to determine the fate between clans. In the middle of this magnificent jungle of waterfalls and rolling mountains in the southeast of the Southern Highlands, in Dokei village around the year 1932, the son of a warrior was born. His mother called him Dekeleba. In those days the news of a young son born was the envy of the enemy tribe and posed a danger to them, so his every movement would be monitored. A mother was allowed to sing her chanting tale to describe the beauty of her new-born child and to give the name she preferred. She believed that her boy would be the hero of his clan.

Dekeleba

My son
My son
You look so beautiful
You are strong and splendid
Your arms are like the birds of the lake
Flying and tweaking above the waters looking out
For its foes and to save those of its own
My son
My son
I will call you Dekeleba, the lake bird.

Warring tribes showed no mercy as tribal fights reached new heights of violence. Word spread that every child and woman had to move through the jungle's back corridors towards Yanguli village while the young and energetic men took on the battle. Dekeleba's father should have done the same but instead he opted to get some food from the gardens as he knew most women and children wouldn't survive the long walk without food. It would take 3 hard days of walking to reach Yanguli.

Dekeleba had to be saved at all cost and this was his father Yonape's central concern. A quick harvesting of vegetables was done while the baby hung in his bilum on a nearby dry branch. But just at that time the enemy was already closing in. However Yonape, being the great warrior of his time, moved swiftly to protect the child. Having seen this action, the mother ran off into the nearby bushes,

the Lake Bird

fleeing for her life. "Woman, don't run away," was Yonape's cry, "come back and pick up the child or it will mean your life". Hesitantly the poor women came back and did as she was commanded.

The battle of a lifetime ensued. Yonape was one of the lucky survivors of the great fight between his tribe, the Dokei Tipurupeke, and the enemy tribe. He fought the fight of a fierce warrior, the enemy couldn't overpower him. The child was saved and they were able to make the journey

Dekeleba

and settle in Yanguli village. Little did Yonape know about his son's future but what this father did became the talking point of his new village, which made him famous among his circle.

Young Dekeleba was being eyed to carry on his father's legacy. Home was far from Yanguli but Yonape never gave up telling his son stories of where he originated from. His father would remind him always that he belonged to Dokei. "That's where your ancestor's spirits are buried, your mountains, valleys, the mighty rivers and the forest which all makes you who you are," he would say.

Settling and growing up in Basabulu in Yanguli was no different however. Like every male child in a patrilineal society it was important for Dekeleba to know his origins right from childhood. The oral passing down of traditions are hard to forget as they are deeply rooted in the clan history. "Like father - like son," was always something that the chiefs in those days would say, ensuring that the son must listen and follow every instruction since it reflected the father.

Dekeleba had to do almost everything he was asked to. All this instruction was good for his upbringing and the values of leadership were instilled in him from a tender age. He was expected to display these even among his peers.

The long Hausman (men's house) or 'halida' was always the place where advice and instruction were taught. It was this instruction that every man and male child was expected to live by. Likewise, every woman and female child was required to stay in separate female houses or 'rante' that were built alongside the Hausman.

the Lake Bird

As Dekeleba was approaching adolescence, an uncle from the distant village of Samberigi visited old Yonape with gifts and brought news of a dead warrior. He asked if Dekeleba's name could be changed to Kitapateke, after the deceased man. This was agreed to and the gifts were accepted followed by Yonape announcing to his household that from this time on his son would be called Kitapateke. Dekeleba would become his hidden or other name.

Father to son instruction and advice were very crucial for a growing young Kitapateke as it made understanding much easier when it came to issues to do with man-hood. Kitapateke always recalled that the advice from his father was purely about respect. Yonape would always tell his son, "do for others what you want them to do for you".

Of all the skills shown to him by his father, hunting became a big part of Kitapateke's life. Special hunting skills were learnt on those long tiring trips taken with his father. This meant he never had time to do other social activities such as ganging up and playing the traditional martial arts, 'harpureande' with youths of the same age.

In those days it wasn't easy as a boy from another tribe because the chances of being caught and brought before the spotlight was high. Even the village laws were tough and penalties were imposed on law breakers and so people were mindful of their conduct. The young people were not allowed to talk to the opposite sex of another tribe because there were strict rules governing this. People in those days used to wear tree bark girdles and tapa cloth so much of their body was exposed but there never arose any sexual desire for the opposite sex as the rules set in place were powerful enough that this was accepted as normal. Young girls were taught the skills of womanhood with strict advice from their mothers.

Kitapateke was most liked by his sisters and aunt for the great skills he displayed in hunting. There was always a variety of surplus meat in their home. These great skills were marvelled at by the villagers. As Kitapateke reached manhood he began to see less of his father going on hunting trips and he knew his medical condition was getting worse. It was on his very last night before old Yonape shut his eyes for good that he called his son over to hear his last words. "My son," he said "I will not say anything new but remember, respect people as they are and follow in my footsteps and strive for peace wherever you live". Kitapateke recognised that obeying his parents was one of the greatest commandments that he would always follow.

Wataka village in the Polupa district

The Dobu Trade

The village people began to see the passion and character of Kitapateke in how he related to people. They eventually involved him as a messenger boy for the first 'luluwai/tultul' from Yanguli village, Mr Tirikai Olawe. By this time, around the 1950's, government officers had begun patrolling parts of the Erave area and were moving in and out of the Kikori Administration Post.

To become a messenger boy one had to know the language of Motu. Kitapateke was fortunate to learn this language during the trading, 'Halame peyaseki' or 'Dobu', as it was commonly known. This took place between the Kairi Rumu of the lower Kikori and the Yanguli people. The traditional barter trade system opened up after

Mr Tirikai Olawe, first Luluai

the settling in of the planters and colonial masters in the Kikori Administration. Government officers patrolling up through Mt Murray began using axes and bush knives to establish pathways, much to the curiosity of the locals who wished to have these superior tools. The locals traditionally used stone axes known as 'sipali', which would take a much longer time to chop down trees, make gardens and gather wood for building houses. The patrol team would include Kairi Rumu men who spoke both Motu and the Kairi language, which was understood by some of the Yanguli men due to their common ancestoral migratory patterns. Eventually the Kairi Rumu men explained that in order to obtain these western items the whiteman needed tobacco or 'soko' in exchange.

The Yanguli men took this business seriously and put 6 months of work into planting, harvesting and processing what was thought to be the most prestiguous crop ever. The tobacco gardens were well cultivated and well managed including proper drainage and fencing to avoid any unnecessary disturbance to their gardens. Typical business factors such as communication, transportation and quality control were crucial to ensure that this business was vibrant and of benefit to everyone. The men would get into the men's longhaus and start sorting out amongst themselves who should take part in the voyage. This discussion included character checks, physical appearance in terms of disability and preference for youthful types. Any differences among themselves had to be reconciled as they would be entering another peoples' territory. Like a team set for a major competition, these factors were crucial to ensure there was a team effort and cohesiveness among the participants.

Young teenagers were asked to be part of the trip to gain experience and to help share the load of carrying their food rations.

It would take almost 10 days to reach the agreed site. A messenger played a vital role much like a middle man in modern times and ensured that the time and location were all agreed upon before the trade eventuated. The Yanguli men would travel the Wamo road whilst the Samberigi men would take the Aku road. It was during these times as a teenager that Kitapateke learnt how to speak Motu as he observed and learned from the bigger boys and menfolk. The men were away for more than a month although there were only 2 days of trading. The actual length of the trip depended a lot on the weather and the many long days of walking there and back. The return of the men was signalled by a big bonfire which was lit at the summit of Mt Murray and the rest of the villagers including the women and children would race up the mountain to welcome the men home. They did not do an actual handshake though or get the items which had been brought back.

Firstly, a spirit removal ceremony that had two parts was normally held to chase out spirits thought to have followed them or caused any sicknesses that were foreign. Huge smoke plumes were created by burning strong wood and all the men involved in the trading trip would take turns in jumping over the hot fire several times until they sweated. As soon as they had crossed over to their home boundaries the second part of the ceremony took place. They then entered the Hausman and stayed there for almost a week in isolation from the rest of the community until the elders gave the nod to indicate that the process was complete. The men were then able to mix around with other members of the community and start the whole process over again.

Families whose husbands and brothers had been on the trip would bring back cooking pots known as billycans, axes known as tomayoks, and the most prized treasure of all which was the red laplap. This was known as calico (normally 2 yards) and sometimes referred to as 'kabugauna' (Yanguli pronunciation), not unlike the Motu expression 'gavamani gauna' or government property. Items obtained depended on the soko bundle which was being traded and on the quantity and quality of it. Strong ties were developed between trading individuals and sometimes this would lead to inter-marriage. Kitapeteke now knew the Motu language and spoke it well. It made him the most favoured candidate as a messenger for the luluwai of the new Erave patrol post now being established. The importance of this station was made clear when about 20 Papuan police officers were stationed there, with the requirement that all villages in the area were to supply able bodied men to be rostered for the work of hand building a large commercial airstrip there.

Arranged Marriage

"It's time for you to get married," was the announcement made by Kitapateke's uncle as Kitapateke returned from a hunting trip. This was in the year 1960. Kitapateke had not known that the marriage arrangements had been made some days earlier.

In those days parents or extended family members chose a future wife based on the character of the young woman. It was always a cultural practice that the boy's parents did the approaching and the girl's parents would wait for those who might be interested in their daughter to approach them.

At other times, special singsing places or 'tupale' became a time of courtship for young people. A young woman was allowed to pull a feather from the head-dress of the man she admired. The man would decide - if he was in agreement he wouldn't reclaim his feather but if he did not agree he would demand it back. Sometimes a commotion would occur amongst the women if several of them admired the same man.

Kitapateke's family negotiated for Nipuluwande Kopono, the daughter of Kopono Tirikai. Her parents were in favour so willingly accepted the bride price. Nipuluwande had the character that every parent would want for their son's wife.

Dekeleba

She was hard working, quiet, humble and obedient to her parents.

Marriage had its own betrothal process that took place over a period of time. Once the agreement was established the first installment of the bride price was paid by the grooms' family. As a sign of the agreement, the bride carried a long hand-woven bag or bilum called 'meiyenu' on her head until the betrothal was over and the final instalment of the bride price paid. This went on for a year during which time she lived in the man's mother's house but was not allowed to see her husband-to-be. During this period the groom was required to hunt for game and supply the bride's family, often living out in the jungle surviving on wild fruits and nuts.

As soon as the bride entered the house, the man's relatives were to do what is known as 'washing her feet'. This was given in the form of gifts such as kina shells and food which was taken by the aunt that accompanied her.

The bride lived in the man's mother's house for almost a year while the man stayed at the hausman. However, if they happened to cross paths mistakenly, the bride would cover her face and body with a laplap or tapa cloth from her head or even take cover by jumping into the nearby bushes as if she had met a ghost. Sometimes the woven bag would become dirty and worn out so it was replaced with a new one. This time was the testing period for the groom. He needed to work hard and prove his worth to his in-laws and the bride would in return bring vegetables and kina shells from her family. In those days the bride price included pigs, tree kangaroos, bundles of kina shells, or 'poi' similar to shells. These shells were valued according to type and quality.

During the final part of the betrothal process, which included the removal of the 'meiyenu' and uniting of the couple, both families would slaughter pigs or any other wild game that was available and cook in the earth oven. The heart of the cooked pork was given on one wooden plate to the new couple and they were told to face each other and start sharing and eating the meat as a sign of uniting. In the old world the process was enduring as it added up to the value of marrying a virgin girl or love being put to the test.

The Lord's Calling

Kitapateke's commitment to being a messenger boy became a job he loved. Even with marital obligations he adamantly continued to carry out his duty. He was paid in the form of a packet of biscuits and a can of fish every time he carried out the job. He did his duties with such diligence that people trusted and liked him.

It was during one of those times at Erave station in 1961 that a visiting missionary, Mr Ian Collingwood, a fundamentalist from the Unevangelized Field Mission (UFM), was there. Mr Collingwood held a crusade for almost a month calling on people to refrain from other spiritual worship and convert to Christianity.

He explained that it would deliver all mankind from oppression and prepare souls for an eternity in heaven and also that other forms of community services could be achieved. Kitapateke was convicted of his need for the Christian faith and accepted Jesus Christ as his personal master and savior through a prayer of faith. Another fellow Yanguli man, Kende Kope who happened to be at Erave also was converted. Both men vowed to reach Yanguli for Christ.

After the crusade was finished Kitapateke wasted no more time in the job he had once loved; rather he journeyed back to Yanguli leaving Kende in Erave and began the mission he wanted to accomplish. With the fire of Christianity burning in him and the desire to spread the word of God, his wife was also converted. She was very supportive and decided to also take up the call to do mission work. They both were able to convert a handful of the Yanguli people.

The front of the Yanguli Hausman was always the centre place for Kitapateke's preaching. However early times seemed pretty tough as criticism was always leveled against the Bible and God. Despite the obstacles the couple managed to get the first group of people converted. They included Miss Touwande Poleye , Mr. Kewe Poleye and wife Sumamenu, Pastor Yalo and wife Andia, Pastor Sawelea and wife. They were also the first to be baptized along with Pastor Kitapateke and his wife.

Around the mid 1950's missionaries Don and Joan Mosely from Unevangelised Fields Mission (UFM) - later named the Asia Pacific Christian Mission (APCM) - settled at Samberigi and began to build the station there. In 1956 Kitapateke heard of this and established close contact with the late Don Mosely.

Missionary Don Mosely

Don was the one who developed the station and served there for a good number of years. Kitapateke asked for missionaries and so Don arranged for Gogodala pastors,

Pastor Daneke and Pastor Koyama from Wasua, Western Province to come. In 1962 the Pastors came with their families. Pastor Daneke and his wife Weisato were sent to Yanguli while Pastor Koyama and his wife Soteyato were sent to Walo village to help new Christians there.

Pastor Daneke & Koyama families

The coming of these pastor families began to motivate the new Christians who were increasingly interested in learning more about the word of God. Kitapateke became a translator for the pastors by translating from Motu language to Sambeleke pi for them. This was his first job in the mission as a 'tanim tok' or translator. He knew the Lord had prepared him ahead of time for this task by giving him the opportunity to learn the Motu language.

It was not easy for these Gogodala missionary pastors settling into a new area. They had to learn a new language and culture and get used to the highland's staple diet of sweet potato, but over time they began to see the hand of God. The good Lord had sent them for a purpose and that was to accomplish the mission of spreading the word of God.

The pastors felt it was time to conduct baptisms for some of the converts and therefore recommended names to the head missionary, the late Don Mosely, in Samberigi. Those baptized would then proceed to the first Bible school in Samberigi. Don Mosely and the newly arrived school teacher Ken Macnaughtan walked over to Yanguli and, with the assistance of these pastors, conducted the first baptisms ever in Yanguli village at the Basabulu river on the 6th December 1964.

It was the emergence of a new phase in preaching on the importance of the death of Jesus Christ and his resurrection, demonstrated through water baptism. In the face of this spiritual renewal, overturning past spiritual lives, warring tribal chiefs began to seek for unity.

Dekeleba

About the same year Kitapateke was blessed with the birth of his first son, Kolowa, a name given by Pastor Daneke in his Gogodala language depicting him as a teacher or preacher. In the following year a new church building was established in Yanguli and Kitapateke was given the job of a deacon.

Samberigi Bible School

The ten Christians that went through water baptism were called to attend the first Bible school in Samberigi in 1965. Kitapateke and his young family, with his first son still a baby, decided to make the move. It came with the painstaking decision of leaving behind families and having the courage to cross enemy borders.

Although Samberigi was only 10km away, tribal differences had created boundaries and strong mental walls of desperation which lead in turn to deep taboos. It meant that enemy tribes were not able to interact with each other. Kitapateke recalled the day when all Yanguli had to gather and bid them farewell. They did this by way of feasting as if they would never see their village again. He quoted the words of the late luluwai Tirikai Olawe "Goodbye folks, you are going there to give up your lives, we may not see you all again (Ya wandehali o etaloe, iki pao homolo pulumi ekime etaloe)". It was an emotional farewell and the group set off, with anxiety, to face the reality of life in Samberigi.

Life was never going to be the same again as Samberigi was unknown to them. The walk took a full day as they had to climb mountains and cross rivers. At every rest spot they even had to ensure that no food debris or leftovers were left behind. These could become an item for a passing enemy to practice sorcery. One thing for certain, which superseded all taboos and uncertainties, was their determination to spread the gospel of Jesus Christ. They believed deep in their hearts that the gospel had the power to penetrate the heart of every man and bring lasting peace.

First ECP church at Yanguli, 1964

The ultimate aim was to end tribal fighting, the boundaries that say Yanguli for Yanguli, or Samberigi for Samberigi, for that matter. Kitapateke and his team went like onward soldiers fulfilling what is said in the scriptures. Among the Yanguli believers, responsibility had to be shared. Kewe Poleye had to remain in Yanguli as deacon for the church replacing Kitapateke. Miss Touwande Poleye did go with the group to Samberigi but became an assistant mid-wife helping the expatriate missionary nurses, Mrs Joan Mosely and the late Miss Vi Walton. In 1968 she was sent to the Port Moresby-Koki church by the mission with Pastor Kalopei and family and was married in Koki church to Lopele Kende Wawi.

the Lake Bird

Life in Samberigi was not the same but it became a home away from home. The missionaries gave the student families a 5 litre bucket of 'kerapi hali' beans for a week to be shared between two families, so that was like 5 buckets a week for the 10 families. In those days people never did proper cultivation so sweet potato was not grown and so they lived on wild yam or 'kenke' as known in the local dialect. There were moments when Nipuluwande remembered with fond memories about all the sweet potatoes in her mum's string bag but there never was a time that she suggested going back home.

During this time Kitapateke was chosen as a prefect for the three years of the training from 1965 -1967. During the work parade times he would lead the male trainees and go about 5 km into the forest to cut the best wood to build their own houses. Other student families that were enrolled at the Bible school included Pastors Pale, Yakaipoko, Mindipa, Bopele, Kope, Kalopei and their wives.

First Bible School student families

Dekeleba

Practical training was a vital part of the school. All student families were dispersed to villages within the Samberigi and Polopa region. They included, Niae, Pawale, Masiki, Sumbutei, Popuareke, Kanakepolu, Sao, Endeliteke, Pawabi, Marorogo, Kerapi, Pupudao, Wapasale and other smaller villages within the Polopa area. There was a moment in which Kitapateke was preaching in Masiki. This village was known for having a spirit house or 'sape ta' for the ritual pouring of blood from the head of an enemy after a tribal fight, usually a Yanguli man. A man shouted and lifted his bow and arrow ready to shoot, thinking Kitapateke would retaliate with the same. However, without saying anything back he lifted his bible and spoke on peace.

Word spread slowly around the tribal villages about this great leader who was willing to play the mediator role and put an end to tribal fighting through the spreading of the gospel. Even in sport he was chosen to lead his team. There was a soccer team which he captained for Hamoteke village and called his team Niae. To this day the village is commonly called Niae. Other skills were learnt during the duration of their studies. They learnt carpentry, first aid, basic stitches and expatriate missionary ladies would teach the trainee's spouses the basics of midwifery.

In 1968 the trainees graduated as pastors and were sent out to various locations. Pastor Kalopei and his family were sent to Port Moresby – Koki church; Pastor Kope and family went to Niae; Pastor Yalo and family went to Waraka whilst Pastor Kitapateke and family were posted to Wopasale/Pukudao in the Polopa area. About the same year, he was blessed with another son, Tapasale, named after a well-known fearful man who once lived in Dokei and usually used cane/rattan to beat trouble makers.

Pastor Kitapateke with the first Polupas to attend a Yanguli convention

Pastor Kitapateke preaching

Life at the Bible School

More buildings were erected through the volunteer services of interdenominational support groups from Australia and New Zealand. Volunteers would come and spend a good deal of time working together with the locals imparting basic skills of survival and skills of how to handle manual machines such as a tractor.

Examples are those like the late Sarasi who drove the station tractor for a long time. The tractor was very useful and made life a lot easier during the early times when the expatriate missionaries were settling in. The tractor, to the wonder of the locals especially children who would think it was the most bizarre thing, would make the children's mums nervous as the children would run towards the hilly mounds to see it passing thru.

Another was Kende Kope who mastered carpentry despite his older age. The missionaries encouraged agriculture and introduced Arabica coffee which soon became a popular cash crop. Soon everyone was planting coffee which is still evident by the many abandoned blocks which can be seen today. It helped provide school fees for children proceeding to high school after attending the mission established pioneer school of Southern Highlands Province. Now the Don Mosely Primary School, it used to

the Lake Bird

Don Mosely teaching in the Bible School

be known as Mt Murray Community school. Others who did irregular trips according to the mission's arrangement included those expatriates who did recordings of cultural singing and preaching sermons done by local trainee pastors. When Kitapateke graduated from the Bible school he was sent to his first posting with two titles: Chairman of Samberigi District (that covers the Samberigi and the Polopa region and parts of Erave) and as the Local church pastor.

SAMBERIGI DISTRICT E.C.P.

Pastor Kitapateke & Nipuluwande.
E.C.P. District Chairman.

First Posting

Wopasale or Pukudao takes about three (3) days to reach. The young father of two started his adventure leaving behind his young boys with their mother back in Yanguli and carried with him only a hammer, spade, axe, nails and first aid. These were vital as he needed to build a house with the community's help. A site near the common burial ground was identified and he was able to bring his family. In those days new pastors did not wait for the community to prepare the place but rather saw that their presence was more of a motivation for the community to come together.

Settling into his new posting was easier due to knowing the Polopa language, making communication much simpler, though it took a while for people to understand why he was there. In 1970, he was again blessed with another son and he named him Yonape after his own father. He usually integrated spiritual development with addressing health issues in relation to first aid. People in those days wore tapa cloth and so personal hygiene was never a subject of importance since they thought it protected them well from cold and rain. A rare flu broke out throughout the region and he feared that his first aid was not sufficient but he sang songs of praise since no deaths were reported. Every Sunday he would read the Holy Bible in the Samberigi language. The Pukudao people were curious to see if they could have the Bible to read in their own language. Mathew 7:7 became a key emphasis in his proclamation of the gospel. So they began to be serious in the Christian faith and keep up with it and, as a prayer point, include the strength to build an airstrip.

After four years, in 1972 it was like prayer had been answered. An expatriate couple, Carol and Neil Anderson of Summer Institute of Linguistics (SIL)/Ukarumpa, arrived to work with the people to do bible translation and build the airstrip.

The Andersons with Ps Katapateke & others at Fukidoa NT celebration

Another mission worker from Wesleyan Church, Pastor Yawijya joined the team. By then Kitapateke had decided to leave and return to Samberigi. It was like he planted the seed and others came along and watered it to grow until Fukidao was able to see the final product of the New Testament translated in Fukidao language and launched in January 2007.

Dekeleba

A moment he would never forget was when an SIL plane touched down in Samberigi and picked up the pastor couple to take them to witness the Polopa language Bible dedication in Fukidao/Wopasale station.

After four years of serving, Kitapateke returned to Samberigi and pastored the Samberigi station church working together with missionaries Ken and Helen Macnaughtan until they left. Their leaving saw the responsibility pass to the nationals to run the affairs of the Evangelical Church of Papua (ECP), now known as the Evangelical Church of Papua New Guinea (ECPNG), for the Samberigi district.

Ken Macnaughtan

Retired

Pastor Kitapateke Yonape retired after 46 years and was formally recognized by the ECPNG church, Samberigi District and the community. On 24th December 2007, in front of a fully packed capacity crowd, he was also awarded a medal by the then Judge Nemo Yalo. He was also awarded a gold plated engraved stone to recognize his contribution to the church and the leadership he portrayed during this period of intense tribal fighting between the Samberigi and the Yanguli people. On this same day, in a moving ceremonial gesture, he passed on his pastoral title to an up-coming young leader, Timothy Limpia of Dagiri village with these words, "Soar your wings high above, like my mother called me Dekeleba but I bore the title 'pastor' and now I entrust it upon you that you will follow the footpath I walked on to carry the light of the gospel".

He is still alive and will live on as the local icon and with the legacy of a traditional true leader who relentlessly served his people to ensure peace was of paramount importance, the centrepeice of society in the Samberigi valley and the entire Polopa region. Today he leads a quiet life blessed with more than 15 grandchildren. Like the lake bird, he soared his wings high and above and continues to promote words of peace and wisdom.

Pastor Kitapateke with Samberigi-Polupa pastors & wives

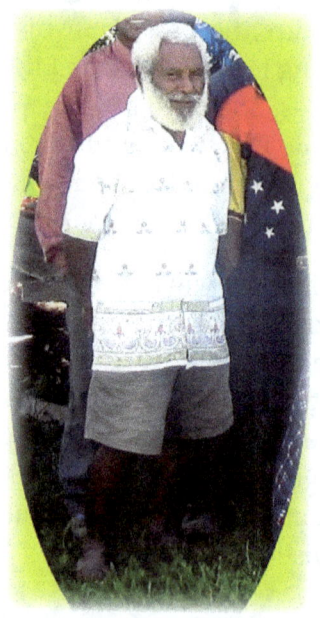

www.ingramcontent.com/pod-product-compliance
Lightning Source LLC
Chambersburg PA
CBHW050322010526
44107CB00055B/2354